DETROIT PUBLIC LIBRARY

3 5674 00204347 0

DETROIT PUBLIC LIBRARY

CHASE BRANCH LIBRARY
17731 W. SEVEN MILE RD.
DETROIT, MI 48235

DATE DUE

BC-3

SIERRA CLUB
WILDLIFE
LIBRARY
BEARS

SIERRA CLUB WILDLIFE LIBRARY BEARS

Text by Ian Stirling

Photographs by Aubrey Lang

General Editor, R. D. Lawrence

CH

Sierra Club Books for Children
San Francisco

The Sierra Club, founded in 1892 by John Muir, has devoted itself to the study and protection of the earth's scenic and ecological resources — mountains, wetlands, woodlands, wild shores and rivers, deserts and plains. The publishing program of the Sierra Club offers books to the public as a nonprofit educational service in the hope that they may enlarge the public's understanding of the Club's basic concerns. The Sierra Club has some sixty chapters in the United States and in Canada. For information about how you may participate in its programs to preserve wilderness and the quality of life, please address inquiries to Sierra Club, 730 Polk Street, San Francisco, CA 94109.

Text copyright © 1992 by Ian Stirling
Illustrations copyright © 1992 by Dorothy Siemens

All rights reserved under International and Pan-American Copyright Conventions. No part of this book may be reproduced in any form or by any electronic or mechanical means, including information storage and retrieval systems, without permission in writing from the publisher.

First edition

All photographs © Aubrey Lang and Wayne Lynch, except the following: © Tom McHugh / The National Audubon Society Collection, 18, 19 (bottom); © Mark Newman, 19 (top), 47; © Ian Stirling, 44.

Library of Congress Cataloging-in-Publication Data

Stirling, Ian.
    Bears / text by Ian Stirling ; photographs by Aubrey Lang ; general editor, R.D. Lawrence. — 1st ed.
        p. cm. — (Sierra Club wildlife library)
    Includes index.
    Summary: Text and photographs introduce the origins, evolution, habitats, behavior, and life cycles of the eight present-day species of bears.
    ISBN 0-87156-574-9 (hardcover)
    1. Bears — Juvenile literature. [1. Bears.]   I. Lang, Aubrey, ill.
II. Title.   III. Series.
QL737.C27S723 1992
599.74'446 — dc20   91-35808

Published in Canada by Key Porter Books Limited, Toronto, Ontario

Printed in Singapore

10 9 8 7 6 5 4 3 2 1

Contents

Watching a Polar Bear   6

Bears of the World   10

The First Bears   25

Small Beginnings   30

Learning About Life   33

Growing Up and Finding a Home   37

What Bears Eat   41

How Bears Communicate   46

Winter Sleep   52

The Future for Bears   56

Index   63

Watching a Polar Bear

Scientists who study bear behavior sometimes spend days in difficult conditions, watching and waiting.

The temperature was thirty degrees below zero as I stood on the cliff in front of my camp, gazing at the windswept ice below. Through the Arctic winter, a bitter wind had blown across the ice ridges, leaving deep drifts of hard snow in its path. That morning, there was only a light wind. Not a sound of another living thing could be heard—no distant birds calling, no arctic foxes barking, nothing. The only noise was an occasional sharp crack as the sea ice shifted slightly with the changing tide.

On the frozen land where I stood, no vegetation was visible above the snow. Before me, the sea ice stretched off into the distance as far as the eye could see. Although the stark scene was beautiful, the penetrating cold was overwhelming. As I shivered in my parka, I wondered how any animal could possibly survive in this hostile environment, especially in winter. Where could it find anything to eat out in that polar wasteland, and how could it keep from freezing to death?

Then, right below me, less than a thousand feet away, was the answer I had come searching for. Looking comfortable and completely at ease, a huge polar bear ambled over the snowdrifts. Its large head swayed slowly from side to side as it walked, and its nose tested each tiny breeze for the scent of a seal. Occasionally it paused to look around, sometimes digging a little snow with the sharp claws on its huge forefeet. Suddenly it lay down, rolled over onto its back, and wriggled around with all four feet waving in the air. It was scratching its back just like my dog at home! Soon afterward, it drifted off to sleep for a while.

A polar bear is entirely comfortable in its icy environment.

I laughed to myself because it looked so comical, but the bear had just taught me an important lesson: For a polar bear, this was not a tough environment but its natural home. With its fur coat and the layer of fat underneath, the bear was perfectly comfortable and completely relaxed. Although I couldn't see anything for it to eat, the bear knew there were lots of seals nearby. It could smell their breathing holes in the ice, even though they often are hidden under crusted snow or snowdrifts.

The bear would stand absolutely still, sometimes for hours, waiting for a seal to come up to breathe at the hole beneath the bear's feet. Slowly the bear would raise its huge body to a standing position and then smash down hard with its front paws, trying to catch the seal before it escaped back down into the sea. Sometimes the hunt would be successful and sometimes not. In either case, the bear just carried on at the same steady, undisturbed pace. If it got sleepy, it lay down on the ice or dug a little pit in a snowdrift and went to sleep. When it woke up, it would continue hunting regardless of the time of day or night. To learn how polar bears live in the Arctic, all I had to do was to be patient and watch. They would tell me everything in their own time and in their own way.

For more than twenty years, people have watched and studied polar bears to learn some of their ways. We have followed them in their travels throughout the year, watched mothers teach their cubs to find seals at different seasons, and enjoyed the sight of cubs at play. In some wonderfully funny moments, we have seen cubs learning to survive in the Arctic environment. One cub, for example, loved to run and make splashing belly-flop dives in pools of sea water on top of the ice in early summer. One day, just as the cub was flying through the air, a young seal surfaced to breathe and practically put its head in the cub's

mouth! The cub was delighted. It gamboled all over the ice with the seal until its mother galloped over, took the seal, and began to eat it. In that moment, the cub learned where food came from. Thereafter, it approached cracks in the ice in a different way.

Through the years, we have learned a lot about how polar bears live in the Arctic. Other scientists have followed grizzly bears or black bears in the north as they went about their lives on the treeless tundra or in the forests of North America, Europe, and Asia. Some bears that live deep in the bamboo forests and subtropical jungles of Asia and South America are still more of a mystery to us. However, humans are rapidly taking over the bears' natural habitats all over the world. If we want wild bears to survive in the future, we need to understand their lives and provide for their needs now.

Polar bear cubs follow their mothers everywhere, learning how to survive.

Bears of the World

Bears, like humans, are mammals. They nurse their young with milk and have hair on their bodies. One group of mammals, the *Carnivora*, have teeth that are specially developed for killing and eating other animals. Among the many carnivores, bears form their own unique family, called the *Ursidae*.

Bears are large and have heavy-built legs and bodies. Each foot has five long, nonretractable claws that are used for digging and climbing. Bears walk flat on their feet like humans do, a type of walking that is called *plantigrade*. (In contrast, dogs and cats walk on their toes; this is called *digitigrade* walking.) Although bears may appear slow and cumbersome, they are remarkably agile. Over short distances, they can run much faster than a person can. Their hearing and sight are thought to be similar to that of humans, but their sense of smell is much better than ours.

Images of bears and stories about these fascinating creatures have influenced people throughout history. Cave drawings of bears that were made more than 10,000 years ago can still be seen in Europe today. Over the centuries, stories about bears have remained popular—bears that talk, bears that turn into princes, bears that eat porridge and sleep in beds, and even bears that go to school.

Because of their large size and enormous strength, bears inspire both fear and respect. When bears were hunted with weapons such as spears or bows and arrows, a person who managed to kill a bear was regarded as a great hunter. Native peoples respected the spirits of animals, and when an animal was hunted and killed, its spirit was honored with special rituals. The spirit of the bear was considered especially powerful, and bear teeth and claws were valued as good-luck charms.

HOW SIMILAR ARE BEARS AND HUMANS?

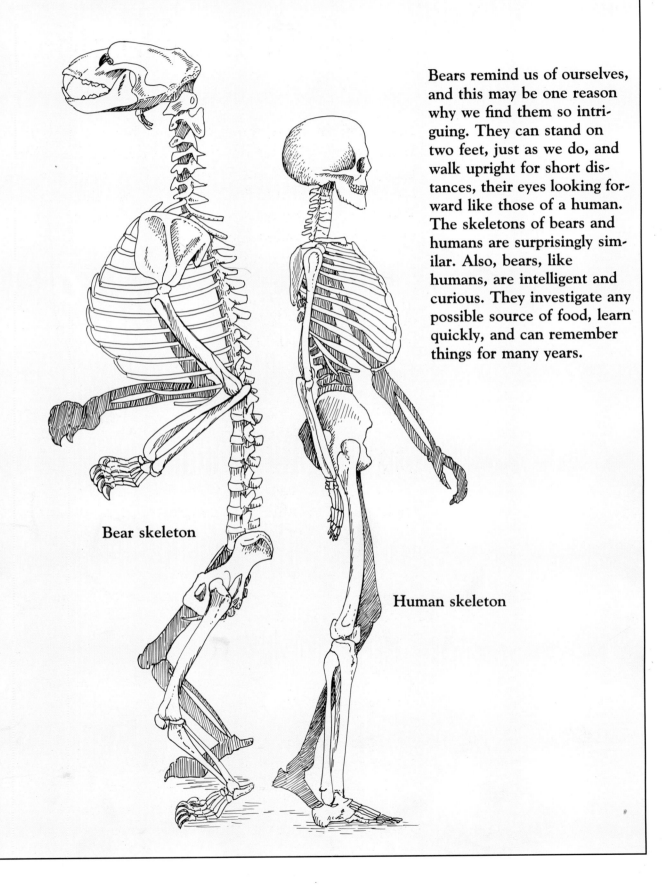

Bears remind us of ourselves, and this may be one reason why we find them so intriguing. They can stand on two feet, just as we do, and walk upright for short distances, their eyes looking forward like those of a human. The skeletons of bears and humans are surprisingly similar. Also, bears, like humans, are intelligent and curious. They investigate any possible source of food, learn quickly, and can remember things for many years.

Bear skeleton

Human skeleton

There are eight different kinds, or *species*, of bears in the world today. They live in a variety of habitats, from the ice fields of the Arctic, to the forests and plains of North America, Asia, and Europe, to the subtropical jungles of Asia and South America. There are no bears in Australia, the Antarctic, or most of Africa.

The distinctively colored panda of southeast China is the easiest bear to recognize. For many years, scientists thought pandas were not true bears but were more closely related to the raccoon family. Now, with more evidence available from new research, they are considered to be in the bear family.

The white polar bear of the Arctic is the largest of the bears. In fact, it's the largest land-living carnivore in the world. Males are much bigger than females, weighing about twice as much. Each year, polar bears walk several thousand miles over the Arctic ice in search of seals. They follow a similar route every year and almost never meet any other kinds of bears.

Polar bears hunt seals and other sea mammals throughout the Arctic.

Pandas are the rarest of bears, living only in a very small area of China.

AVERAGE SIZES AND WEIGHTS OF BEARS

Panda
male: 220 lb.
female: 185 lb.

Sloth bear
male: 240 lb.
female: 220 lb.

Polar bear
male: 990 lb.
female: 550 lb.

Sun bear
male: 110 lb.
female: 100 lb.

Grizzly bear
male: 770 lb.
female: 500 lb.

Asiatic black bear
male: 240 lb.
female: 165 lb.

American black bear
male: 285 lb.
female: 175 lb.

Spectacled bear
male: 330 lb.
female: 240 lb.

The grizzly bear got its name because of the lighter-colored hairs on its back and shoulders, which give the bear a "grizzled" appearance.

The next largest bears are the coastal grizzlies of British Columbia and Alaska. Grizzly bears got their name because they have lighter-colored hairs in their coat, giving them a "grizzled" appearance from a distance, like a person whose dark hair has become streaked with gray. Grizzly bears are also called "brown bears" in Europe and Asia and in some parts of Alaska, but they are all the same species. In North America, there are two forms (or *subspecies*) of grizzlies, which differ in size and live in different areas. The larger form, the coastal grizzly, feeds on the abundant salmon that swim upstream to spawn. The smaller form of grizzly lives in the interior of western Canada, Alaska, and parts of northwestern Montana. One particularly famous group of grizzlies lives in Yellowstone National Park. Although some live in forests, grizzlies seem to prefer open country such as the Arctic tundra or meadows high in the mountains above the tree line.

The black bear is the most widespread and abundant bear in North America.

The American black bear is probably the best-known bear in the world. Although black is the usual color of this species, "black bears" may be brown, and cinnamon-colored individuals are not unusual. In the interior of Alaska, there are some that are a light bluish gray. And in one small area on the west coast of British Columbia, there are even "black bears" that are white! A mother may have cubs of different colors in the same litter. Black bears prefer to live in the forest where cubs can climb trees to escape enemies such as grizzlies, who rarely climb. The mother bear can then run away by herself, returning later to retrieve her cubs. The only place where black bears live in treeless country is northern Labrador, where there are no grizzlies.

BLACK BEAR OR GRIZZLY?

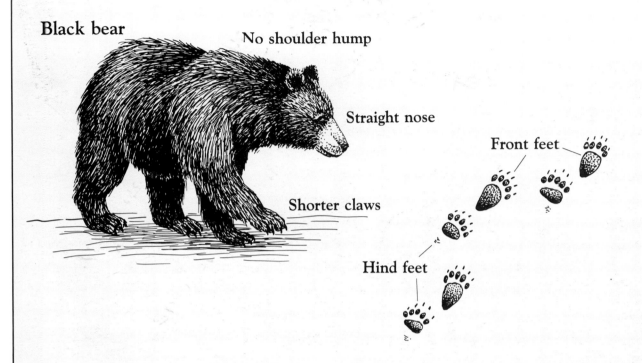

Black bear

No shoulder hump

Straight nose

Shorter claws

Front feet

Hind feet

Front feet

Hind feet

Grizzly bear

Shoulder hump

Dish-shaped face

Longer claws

You can't tell a black bear from a grizzly bear by color alone — or by size. There are lighter and darker, larger and smaller individuals in both species. You can tell them apart if you see them in profile. The grizzly bear has a shoulder hump and a dish-shaped face. The black bear lacks the hump and has a straighter nose.

Because grizzlies have such large, long claws, the claw marks show up more in their tracks than in black bears' tracks. In addition, their toes are farther apart than those of black bears.

*The sun bear is the smallest
species of bear in the world.*

The Asiatic black bear is found in southern and eastern Asia. It is similar in appearance to its closely related North American cousin, but relatively little is known about it.

Finally, there are three species of small black-colored bears that live in subtropical jungles. The spectacled bear lives mainly in the rain forests of the Andes mountains in South America, although some are found in the inland deserts as well. The sloth bear lives in the jungles of India, Pakistan, and Sri Lanka. The smallest and least-known bear in the world is the sun bear, which lives in the lowland forests of southeast Asia. Although these subtropical species once lived in a fairly large area, they were never plentiful in any part of their range. Because these bears have been hunted intensively, few are left in most places. They usually avoid people and are active mainly at night in thick forests where they are difficult to watch. As a result, we know relatively little about any of them.

Asiatic black bears are smaller than North American ones, but their ears are bigger.

Sloth bears specialize in eating ants and termites.

19

THE EIGHT SPECIES OF BEAR

Sun bear

Spectacled bear

Polar bear

American black bear

Panda

Grizzly bear

Asiatic black bear

Sloth bear

Polar bear

Grizzly bear

Spectacled bear

American black bear

Sloth bear

Asiatic black bear

Panda

Sun bear

WHERE BEARS LIVE

The spectacled bear is the only
bear that lives in South America.

24

The First Bears

Fossils of the earliest bear indicate that it was a small, doglike creature, about the size of a fox terrier. It lived more than twenty million years ago in what is now Europe. Scientists call this early bear *Ursavus elmensis*, the "dawn bear." Ursavus had sharp canine teeth like a dog but, like most modern bears, its back teeth, or molars, were fairly flat for chewing vegetation.

Although there are only eight species of bears in the world today, more species existed in the past. They lived all over the world, except in Australia and Antarctica. The remains of several living and extinct species of bears have been found in caves in Europe, Asia, and North America. For example, fossils tell us that within the last million years or so, the Florida cave bear—which was as large as the present-day coastal grizzly—lived all over what is now the southern United States, from California to Georgia and Florida. As time passed and environmental conditions changed, many species became extinct (no longer living anywhere on earth) for reasons that we often don't understand.

Fossils of most species of bear are rare, but there is one truly remarkable exception—the extinct cave bear of Europe. A large number of fossilized bones of the cave bear have been found in caves throughout Europe. In one cave, there are bones from 30,000 to 50,000 individual bears! Cave bears thrived about 300,000 years ago. They may have lived as recently as 35,000 years ago and may have been hunted by early people called Neanderthals who lived in Europe at that time. Why the European cave bear died in these caves in such large numbers over so many years remains a mystery.

The long neck of the polar bear is useful for reaching down into cracks and breathing holes in the ice to catch seals.

One of the most incredible bears was the giant short-faced bear that lived on the western plains of North America. It had a massive body, probably twice the size of a grizzly. Its legs were unusually long for a bear, so it probably could run much faster than any bear alive today. It was the largest land mammalian carnivore the world has ever known—and probably the most ferocious. The giant short-faced bear is extinct now, but fossilized bones that are only 11,000 years old were found near Lubbock, Texas. Those remains have marks on them that were made by the weapons of humans. We don't know whether the humans killed the bears or whether they were trying to cut bones from animals that died naturally. However, it seems unlikely that these first people in the southwestern United States hunted such a huge and powerful creature as the short-faced bear. They are more likely to have lived in danger of being hunted themselves.

The newest species of bear is the polar bear. Based on genetic studies, scientists think the first polar bears may have appeared as recently as a million years ago. The earliest-known fossil is only about 100,000 years old. Polar bears evolved from grizzly bears, possibly along the Arctic coast of Siberia. They seem to have developed very quickly, taking advantage of the abundance of seals that no other land carnivore was hunting. Their bodies became adapted to the Arctic environment in several ways. The most obvious adaptation is their white coat that camouflages them in the snow and ice. But beneath the white fur lies a surprise: The skin of a polar bear is black. This is another adaptation to life in the Arctic. The dark skin readily absorbs heat from the sun once the heat

The thick coat of the polar bear helps to keep it warm and makes it hard to see against the snow.

THE BEAR FAMILY TREE

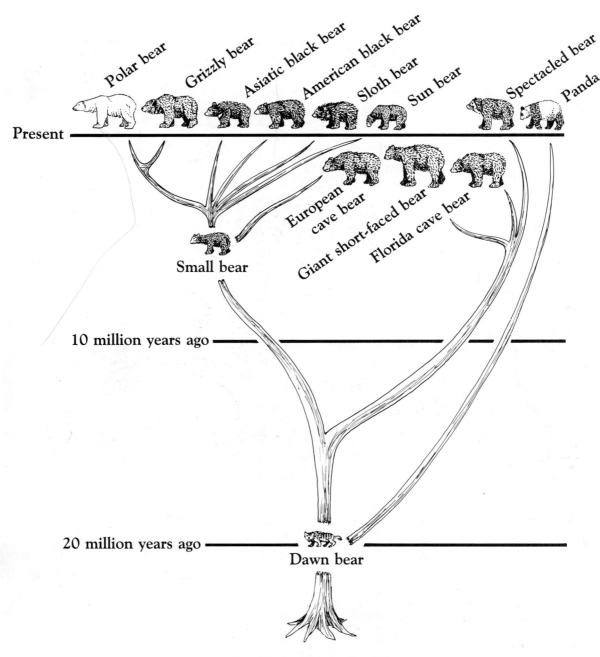

This family tree shows the eight species of modern bears and a few of the extinct species. Of the eight living bear species, six are quite closely related. And of those six, the polar bear and the grizzly bear are the closest relatives.

is reflected down through the fur. Also, polar bears' necks became longer and slimmer, so they could reach into the cracks and holes in the ice where seals breathe. Their feet grew huge, becoming better paddles for swimming. When polar bears walk on thin ice, their large feet also act like snowshoes to prevent them from breaking through the ice crust.

In the wild, polar bears and grizzly bears do not meet during the mating season, because they live in completely different habitats. But if they are housed together in a zoo and allowed to mate, the bears can produce cubs that are capable of having cubs themselves when they are grown. This ability to interbreed shows how closely related these two species are.

The paw of a polar bear has fur between the pads to help keep the feet warm and to keep the bear from slipping on the ice.

Small Beginnings

A black bear cub climbs over its mother before venturing outside.

Although full-grown bears are large and fearsome in appearance, they do not start out that way. Their cubs are surprisingly small and helpless when they are first born, especially in comparison to the size of their mothers. For example, a newborn grizzly bear or polar bear weighs only about a pound and a half at birth — a fraction of the size of an average newborn human. Its mother, at four to five hundred pounds, is three to four hundred times heavier than her cub. By comparison, the mothers of most other newborn mammals, including humans, are only fifteen to twenty times heavier than their offspring.

All the North American bears (black, grizzly, and polar) breed in the late spring. The male and female stay together for a week or more during mating, but afterward they live independently. The male does not help at all in raising the cubs and, in fact, may hunt and kill them if he has an opportunity.

In the middle of winter, female black bears and grizzly bears give birth to their cubs in a den dug into the ground. Female polar bears do the same, but their maternity dens are more likely to be in a snowdrift. The temperature in the den may be only a few degrees above freezing. The cubs' eyes are closed at first, and their hair is so fine that they look naked. They are quite helpless for several weeks. During this period the mother sits or lies on her side in the den and keeps her cubs warm by cuddling them close to her body. In the thick hair on her stomach are nipples from which the tiny cubs can drink the rich milk she produces. The cubs grow quickly. In a few weeks, they open their eyes and begin to move about in the den. As they play and explore their surroundings, they scratch and dig and poke at the walls and floor.

Most females give birth to more than one cub at a time. In polar bear and grizzly bear births, twin litters are most common—they occur about two-thirds of the time. Most other litters have only one cub, but occasionally there are triplets. Litters of four cubs are rare among polar bears and grizzly bears, but they have occurred. Sometimes in the eastern United States, if food is abundant, black bears may have four, five, or even six cubs. But even in good years, some of the cubs in such large litters may die because the mother simply can't find enough for all of them to eat.

In the spring, the mother takes her cubs out of the den so they can play near the entrance. After being cooped up in such a small space for three months or so, they need exercise to make them strong enough to follow their mother in search of food. Bear cubs that are born in the northern mountains or in the Arctic also have to adjust to the cold after being inside a comfortable den. At first, they play beside the entrance under the watchful eye of their mother.

Grizzly bears mate in May and June.

It's a big world out there!

Periodically they return to her, have a drink of milk, and curl up together for a nap. Later, they make trips of a few hundred yards, returning regularly to the security of the den. They still sleep inside the den at night or during periods of bad weather. While they are outside, the mother may dig about in search of plants from the previous season that might still be edible, but mostly she just watches out for the safety of her cubs. She rests while keeping a careful eye on the surroundings, and retreats to the den at any sign of danger. After a week or two of this gentle exercise, the cubs are ready to leave the den and learn how to fend for themselves. By that time, the mother has used up most of her stored fat, and she needs to find food.

Learning About Life

Bear cubs spend a long time with their mothers, for very good reasons. It takes a long time for them to get big enough to protect themselves against other animals, such as wolves or larger bears. But growing large enough is only part of the explanation. A bear needs to know many different things to survive, and it cannot rely on instinct alone to know what to do. A cub must be taught, and its mother is the teacher. Black bear cubs stay with their mothers for a year and a half; grizzly and polar bear cubs stay with their mothers for two and a half years — sometimes longer.

Think about what a cub must learn to survive! First is the challenge of diet! Most bears eat different foods in spring, summer, and fall. Their food may be plants or insects, and they sometimes kill and eat birds or mammals. But bears will also eat dead animals they find. They must remember that something is good to eat even if they have seen it only once before. Also, the supply of berries or acorns can change greatly from year to year. If something is not available where it was last year, what does a bear do next?

As they watch their mother, the grizzly cubs learn to eat sedges that grow along the water's edge.

Two grizzly cubs sit still and watch intently to see how. . .

Foods that are common in one area, such as Pennsylvania, may not even exist in another, such as Alaska. Cubs need to learn not only what things are edible, but where to find them, and when. All these things are learned by watching, then imitating, their mothers.

For example, when polar bear cubs first go out onto the sea ice, they stay close behind their mothers and watch. They must learn where to find seals, how to catch them, and what to do after a seal is caught. The cubs quickly learn to recognize when their mother is interested in a crack in the ice or a breathing hole

34

where a seal might appear. She "freezes" on the spot and watches intently, staying motionless for several minutes at a time. This is a signal for the cubs to stop walking, lie down, and be still. Then the female creeps forward and silently lies down beside the breathing hole to wait for the seal to surface. Noise or movement might scare it away. If the cubs get impatient and approach their mother, she gives them a firm swat with her large paw to tell them they did the wrong thing. If no seal comes, the female ambles on to find another place to hunt while the cubs sniff about and investigate the spot she left. When the cubs are a

35

little older, they will pick a similar spot and lie down to wait on their own.

As the cubs grow, they begin to hunt regularly, although they rarely catch anything. Even after two and a half years, when they are about to become independent, young polar bears catch seals much less frequently than their mothers do. By that time, though, they have been watching and practicing for long enough to survive on their own.

As the seasons pass, a bear needs to know where to go next. If there is food in a particular location one year, a bear is likely to return there at the same time the next year. But there is much to discover besides where to find the next meal. Which animals are dangerous and should be avoided? What is the best thing to do in bad weather? What makes one place better than another for the winter's sleep? It's easy to see why the mother bear's teaching is so important. The cubs' survival depends on learning as much as they can about the area they live in. There is no playing hookey in this school! Cubs that fail to learn simply don't survive.

Polar bears sometimes "freeze" for hours, waiting to catch a seal.

Growing Up and Finding a Home

The most difficult period for any bear is the first year of independence after leaving its mother. Young bears are less experienced at finding food. And because young bears are relatively small, larger animals may keep them away from the best feeding areas. Sometimes bigger bears even take hard-earned food away from smaller ones. Young bears also face the challenge of finding and defending their own individual territories.

Like most mammals, bears tend to establish themselves within a specific area. Once settled, a bear will live its entire life within the boundaries of this "home range," an area big enough to provide for all the needs it might have from year to year. These needs include food in spring, summer, and fall; safe denning sites for the winter sleep; and mates in the breeding season.

Finding a place to live may be easier for young females than for males. Sometimes black bear mothers make room in their own territories for their daughters to establish themselves as they grow up. Male cubs are not so lucky. They usually have to travel to a new area and then compete with other bears to establish themselves.

Different species require home ranges of different sizes. For example, the average size of the home range of a male panda is only 3.2 square miles, while a male grizzly bear in the Brooks Range of Alaska makes his home in about 271 square miles.

The home ranges of polar bears are far larger than those of any other species, and they are shared with other polar bears. That is because of the unpredictable nature of their sea ice habitat. From year to year, the seals move around, and so do the good hunting spots. Polar bears travel much more than other bears in search of food, and several bears may hunt in the same general area if seals are abundant. In some parts of the Arctic, the home range of an adult female polar bear can be more than 77,500 square miles! (We have data only about female polar bears. The reason is that male polar bears have necks that are wider than their heads, and the radio collars used for tracking their movements—see box on facing page—simply fall off.)

A male polar bear wrestles another to defend his territory.

TRACKING BEARS BY SATELLITE

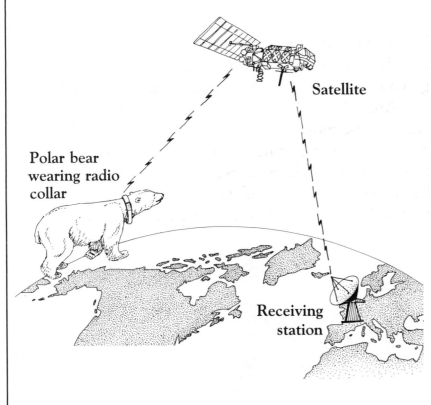

Polar bear wearing radio collar

Satellite

Receiving station

Polar bears travel in distant and dangerous places where humans cannot follow. Scientists can track their movements by attaching radio collars to the bears. The radios send signals to a satellite, which in turn beams the signals to an international receiving station in southern France. From there the information is sent back to the scientists. When the data is entered into a computer program, the computer draws a map of each bear's path. Some bears travel over vast areas of the Chuckchi Sea, visiting both Alaska and the Soviet Union.

Home ranges also vary in size for the same species. In the mountains of western Canada, for example, where food is scarce, the home ranges of grizzlies are four or five times larger than they are in the food-rich area of Kodiak Island in Alaska. The home ranges of male and female bears usually overlap, but, except in the case of polar bears, those of members of the same sex normally do not. If a resident bear finds an intruder of the same sex in its home range, it will usually try to run it off. The home ranges of males are generally larger than those of females of the same species. This is mainly because adult male bears often mate with more than one female, so they try to have their home range overlap the ranges of several females, if possible.

HOW CAN YOU TELL THE AGE OF A BEAR?

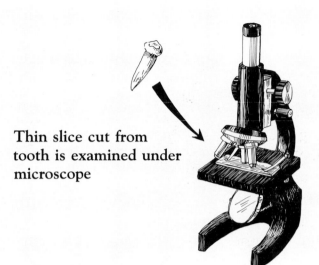

Thin slice cut from tooth is examined under microscope

5 years old
4 years old
3 years old
2 years old
1 year old

Five layers indicate that bear is five years old

Each year, a thin layer of bone is added to the outside of the root of each tooth in a bear's jaw. Just as you can tell the age of a tree by counting the rings in its trunk, you can tell the age of a bear by counting the annual layers in its teeth. To do this, a scientist pulls a small unused tooth out of a bear's lower jaw. (Bears possess some "vestigial" teeth that they don't use.) The tooth is softened in a chemical bath for a couple of days, then a thin slice is cut from it with a very sharp knife. When the scientist looks through a microscope at the slice of tooth he or she can see the layers and count them.

Bears grow rapidly when they are young. They reach maturity some time between five and eight years of age, depending on the species. At maturity, females usually mate and begin to have cubs of their own. Male bears must compete intensely for mates, and a male must be nearly full size before he can compete successfully in these fierce fights. As a result, males are usually several years older than females before they get a chance to breed for the first time.

Bears are long-lived animals. Wild bears in North America normally live to twenty years of age or beyond, with females living longer than males. The oldest wild female polar bear ever found was thirty-two years old. In zoos, polar bears have lived to be more than forty years old.

What Bears Eat

Most species of bears will eat almost anything because their teeth are adapted for eating both plants and animals. They grind up plant material using the large, flat surfaces of their cheek teeth (molars). With their big, sharp canine teeth, they can kill other animals and tear them apart. They also eat the remains of animals that are already dead.

Animals such as wolves that hunt and kill other animals are called *carnivores*. The term comes from two Latin roots: *carn*, meaning "flesh," and *vore*, meaning "eater." Animals such as deer that eat only plants are called *herbivores*. *Omnivores* eat both plants and animals.

Black bears and grizzly bears are omnivorous, and the variety of food they eat is astounding. In the spring, when they first come out of their dens, they eat grasses, berries left over from the previous fall, the soft roots and stems of fleshy plants, the bark of young trees, and fresh leaves.

In summer, the black bears and grizzlies supplement their diet with tiny animals such as insects. Individual beetles, ants, and termites are small food items for such big animals, but bears can eat large numbers of them at anthills or beehives. The larvae of ants and bees are also a nutritious delicacy. And, of course, black bears are famous for liking honey, whether it comes from the honey tree of wild bees or from a farmer's beehive.

Toward autumn, when black bears and grizzlies are fattening up before their winter's sleep, they seek out such things as berries and nuts. These are very rich foods and are often abundant in small areas. The bears can feed intensely and get quite fat in only a few weeks.

Black bears and grizzlies also hunt and kill other animals. On the coast of Alaska and British Columbia, grizzly bears feed on salmon that migrate into the rivers to spawn. At McNeil Falls in Alaska, people come to watch, from a close but safe area, large numbers of these bears fishing. Grizzlies use their strength and large claws to dig marmots and ground squirrels out of their underground burrows. Both kinds of bears are skillful predators of deer fawns, and the calves of elk, moose, and caribou. Grizzlies, which are larger, sometimes kill adult moose, elk, caribou, and musk oxen as well.

Black bears occasionally prey on mammals as large as deer.

Compared to grizzlies and black bears, which eat an extraordinarily varied diet, pandas are extremely fussy. More than ninety-nine percent of their diet consists of bamboo stems and leaves. Their cheek teeth are wider and flatter than those of other bears, an adaptation that helps in crushing the woody stems of bamboo.

The sloth bear of India and Sri Lanka specializes in feeding on insects such as termites. These bears have especially large claws that help them break through the hard surfaces of termite mounds. They are missing the *incisors*, the middle two teeth in the upper jaw. This makes it possible for them to make a funnel with their lips and tongue and suck in large numbers of termites like a vacuum cleaner. Although their mouths are specialized for eating insects, sloth bears also feed on fruits, flowers, and honey.

Pandas eat as much as forty pounds of bamboo a day.

43

The spectacled bear of South America and the sun bear of southeast Asia are especially good climbers and often feed high up in the trees on fruits and soft leaves at the ends of branches. Sometimes they use broken branches to make beds up in the trees and sleep there between meals. Both bears also eat insects and small mammals when they are available.

Polar bears are the most carnivorous bears. They live almost entirely on ringed seals. A ringed seal weighs only about 100 pounds, so it is easy prey for such a large bear. Polar bears can kill larger species, too, such as bearded seals, walruses, and sometimes even small arctic whales weighing up to 1,300 pounds. Because of their animal diet, the molars of the polar bear are sharper and more adapted for cutting and shearing than those of other species of bears.

In some parts of the polar bear's range, there is no ice in summer, so the bears must spend some time on shore. While they are on land, polar bears will occasionally eat some grass or berries, or seaweed washed up along the beach. Usually they eat very little, just resting and living on their body fat, waiting for the ice to form so they can hunt seals again.

Ringed seals, which are abundant in the Arctic, are a favorite prey of polar bears.

The polar bear uses its acute sense of smell to catch seals when they pause to breathe at a crack in the ice.

How Bears Communicate

Some animals, such as wolves who live in packs, need to communicate with one another constantly. Wolves also need to send information over distances, so they howl to one another. Probably because bears tend to live by themselves, they do not have very many ways of communicating. Still, they do have ways of sending messages to other bears.

When two bears come within sight of each other, they communicate by acting in specific ways. For example, if they meet by chance in the forest or at a food source, they signal whether they plan to attack, retreat, or coexist. The size of a bear is in itself a signal; smaller bears will usually avoid or run away from larger ones. Bears of similar size may approach each

This black bear cub is calling for its mother.

Asiatic black bears have a larger white patch than American black bears do.

other and then slowly circle around while they assess who might be bigger and stronger. The way a bear holds its head, ears, and mouth is also a signal. A bear that is about to attack will usually lower its head, flatten its ears back, and face its opponent. It may give a threatening vocalization such as a woof, a snort, or a growl. Sometimes a bear will bluff by starting a threatening charge but stopping well before reaching its opponent.

The black and white markings on the panda and on the face of the spectacled bear are probably helpful for signaling their presence to other bears. But most bears have fairly drab color patterns, and because of

The sun bear has a white patch on its chest and a light-colored muzzle.

this, a bear walking in the woods on all four feet may be difficult for humans to see until they are quite close. However, the black bears of the North American and Asian forests, and the small black-colored bears of the subtropical jungles, have distinct white patches on their chests that contrast sharply with the rest of their fur. Because of this, if one of those bears stood up on its hind feet and faced you, the vivid pattern of the white patch against the black fur would be noticeable immediately. Grizzly bears, which tend to prefer a more open habitat, are already easy to see and do not need color patterns in their fur to draw attention to themselves.

Bears do not vocalize a great deal but they do make some sounds. Mothers and cubs of all species call to one another from time to time if they become separated. Occasionally a bear makes a threatening sound, such as a snort or a woof, to warn another animal that it is getting too close. The forest bears call to one another more often than do the bears of the open country. This is probably because the trees prevent them from seeing one another as easily. For example, the forest-dwelling black bears call more often and with a wider variety of sounds than the grizzlies. Pandas, which live in junglelike bamboo forests, make about ten different kinds of sounds. Similarly, the sun bear and sloth bear are both quite vocal in their jungle habitat. In contrast, the polar bear, which lives in the most open habitat of any bear, gives very few calls. Cubs and their mothers make bawling sounds to each other if they become separated. Males threaten each other with "chuffing" sounds, like coughing or blowing, that cannot be heard very far away.

Black bears and grizzly bears seem to have other ways of communicating, as well. They stand up on their hind feet and reach up as high as they can with their front claws to put deep scratches in the bark of trees. Sometimes near salmon streams there are as many as three or four of these clawed trees per half-mile of trail. The same trees may be marked by different bears. The reason for this behavior is not completely understood, but scientists think it indicates the territory or the status of a particular bear.

When danger threatens, a cub climbs a tree and waits for its mother's signal that it is safe to come down.

On a few special bear trails, all the bears that pass by step in exactly the same footprints year after year.

The use of scents to mark territories or give other information is common in mammals. For example, near their eyes, male deer have glands that they rub on the ground to leave chemical messages for other males. Wolves urinate to mark the boundaries of their territories. Bears have an acute sense of smell, so they probably use special body scents to send messages to other bears. We see bears do things that may send scent messages. For example, grizzly and black bears sometimes rub their bodies against particular trees without marking them with their claws. Occasionally, they rub on the ground as well. Other bears sniff with interest at these spots, but we don't know what they learn there.

In Denali National Park in Alaska, and on the west coast of British Columbia, scientists have found short sections of trail where each grizzly that passes steps in exactly the same spot when it walks by. This must mean something to the bears, but humans don't yet understand it. Why they do this is a mystery — one to be solved by scientists in the future.

BEAR OR RACCOON?

Red panda
(a relative of the raccoon)

Raccoon

Panda

Pandas were once thought to be more closely related to raccoons than to bears. Raccoons, which live only in North and South America, are skilled at handling food with their front paws. Pandas can also manipulate things skillfully with their front paws.

The red panda, a close relative of the raccoon, lives in the same area of the world where pandas live. Both pandas and red pandas have large heads with strong jaw muscles and teeth suitable for grinding vegetation. These similarities suggested that they were related and led to their similar names.

For many years, scientists classified the panda as a member of the raccoon family. Later, as more research was done, scientists looked at the overall shape of the body and examined the skull and teeth of pandas. This led them to recognize the physical similarities between pandas and bears. They also took into account the fact that panda cubs are tiny compared to the size of the mother, and this is characteristic of all bear species. Recently, genetic studies have confirmed that pandas are definitely bears.

Winter Sleep

Grizzlies and black bears face a special problem in winter. The weather becomes much colder, and the lush plants and berries that they feed on stop growing and dry up. Snow may cover the ground for several months. Insects and many small mammals disappear or become difficult to find.

Unlike birds, bears cannot migrate thousands of miles to feeding areas in the south and then return in spring when food is available again. Instead of trying to go somewhere else, bears stay in their own home ranges and eat as much food in the fall as they possibly can. They get fatter at this time of year than at any other. Eventually, just before winter, the ever-shortening days signal that it's time to find a den.

Bears can make suitable dens in a variety of places. The most common place is in a creek bank or hillside, where they dig a small cave with a narrow entrance tunnel. Some dens are dug under trees where the roots can hold the roof together and keep it from falling in. Hollow trees, natural caves, or even a culvert (large pipe) under a road are also suitable sites. The den must be large enough for the bear to move and occasionally stretch a little, but small enough that it can be kept warm with heat from its body. In colder areas, a blanket of snow over the top of the den provides valuable extra insulation. Dens are usually hidden from view and are sometimes in specific areas where the bears don't go at other times of the year.

Among polar bears, only pregnant females enter a snow den for the winter, as they need shelter for their tiny newborn cubs. Other polar bears don't need to sleep all winter, because food remains available.

They can hunt seals out on the frozen sea ice. Even so, they may make temporary dens in the snow during long periods of cold or stormy weather when the seal hunting is poor.

Once a bear is in its den for the winter, its only source of energy for the next few months is the fat stored in its body. It must conserve energy in every way possible, so the bear lies quietly and sleeps a lot. Although it appears groggy, its eyes are open when it is awake and it is aware of what is going on around it. Because the body is a little cooler and the bear is not active, it burns less energy. This helps to make the stored fat last longer.

A polar bear can escape a few days of bad weather by lying down and sleeping in a sheltered spot.

Black bears and grizzlies may dig a den into a hillside . . .

This slowed-down condition of bears in their winter dens is called *carnivore lethargy*, or sometimes just *winter sleep*. It has been called hibernation as well, but research has shown that bears do not actually hibernate. In true hibernators—ground squirrels or marmots, for example—the body temperature drops to only a few degrees above freezing. If true hibernators are disturbed, it takes them a couple of hours to wake up. But sleeping bears in dens are still alert and aware of their surroundings, and they can rouse themselves right away if necessary. This is important for females, who must remain alert to care for their tiny cubs, keeping them warm and nursing them. Because most bear dens are close to the surface of the ground, their occupants may need to move quickly to protect themselves from predators such as wolves or larger bears.

Bears also differ from the true hibernators in another amazing way. Once in its den, a bear maintains

. . . or under a large rock.

itself completely on its stored body fat. Its body obtains the energy it needs, makes its own water, and recycles its waste products. This means that the bear does not drink, urinate, or defecate for several months. When it leaves its den in the spring, much thinner than it was in the fall, these normal body processes begin again. True hibernators such as the ground squirrel, though they also have no need to eat or drink, cannot recycle their waste products. Several times during the winter, ground squirrels must warm up, rouse themselves, eliminate wastes, and then go back to sleep.

Black bears can enter into this special type of sleep only in the late fall, just before the winter begins. If a black bear were kept without food in summer, it would starve. Polar bears, however, can enter into the "winter sleep" state at any time of the year if food becomes unavailable. This remarkable adaptation helps the polar bear survive periods of food shortage in the unpredictable Arctic habitat.

The Future for Bears

For centuries, people have hunted bears and have competed with them for space. At first, the impact of humans was limited, because they had only primitive weapons and they could clear only a limited amount of land. Even so, the European brown bear was already extinct in Denmark about 5,000 years ago, and in Britain about 1,000 years ago.

With the invention of modern rifles, it became easy to kill bears. All over the world, bears were shot for food, for their hides, and for the protection of crops and domestic animals. Often they were killed simply because people feared them.

When Europeans first came to settle in North America, grizzlies were abundant over most of the great plains and mountains from Alaska to Mexico. In the early 1800s, one explorer counted 220 grizzlies along the Arkansas River in a single day. In only one year, 1871, the Hudson's Bay Company bought 750 grizzly hides at their trading post in the Cyprus Hills of southern Alberta.

Over the last hundred years or so, the human population has increased enormously, and vast areas of wild land have been taken over for farms and cities. In the western United States, the number of grizzlies was reduced from about 100,000 in the 1850s to fewer than 1,000 only fifty years later. In California, where the grizzly is pictured on the state flag, grizzlies have been wiped out. They have vanished from the prairie provinces of Canada and from forty-seven of the forty-eight states of the continental United States. They remain only in Alaska, the mountains of western Canada, and the tundra of the central Canadian Arctic.

Grizzly bears need a large wild territory in which to forage and raise their young.

WHERE GRIZZLY BEARS LIVE

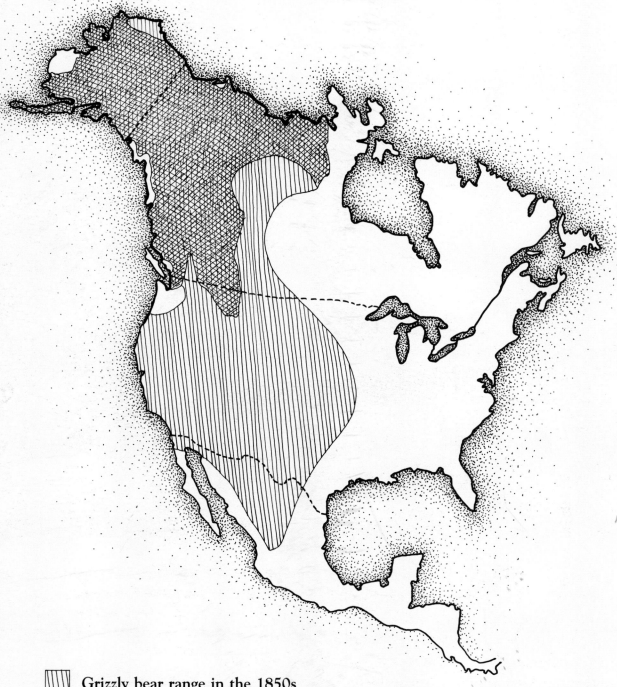

Grizzly bear range in the 1850s

Grizzly bear range today

Until the mid-1800s, grizzly bears were found throughout most of the western half of North America. Today they remain only in north-western Montana, western Canada, and Alaska.

All species of bears have been affected by humans in some way. They have died out in more than half the areas where they used to live. The long-term survival of all the subtropical bears is of urgent concern, because their habitat is being cleared at such a rapid rate. Also, many of these bears are being killed merely so that some of their parts can be used in traditional medical treatments. In addition, teeth and claws are made into necklaces and sold as good-luck charms. Such practices are particularly threatening to the survival of the small bears in southeastern Asia. In many countries, killing bears is illegal, but the laws are difficult to enforce.

Bears that feed in garbage dumps lose their fear of humans and may behave aggressively. Bears are sometimes killed if people feel threatened.

59

CAMPING IN BEAR COUNTRY

Traveling safely in bear country requires a few precautions. Hang your food packs at night where bears can't reach them. Don't keep food in your tent, and *never* feed bears. If you see signs of bears, such as fresh tracks or freshly dug-up ground, you might decide to hike somewhere else that day. Bears can be dangerous if they are startled, so try to make some noise when you are hiking, especially in places where a bear might not hear you or see you until you were very close. If we consider bears' needs as well as our own, we can safely share the wilderness with them.

The future of the panda is another special concern. There are now fewer than 1,000 left, in six groups living in different areas. Some of these groups are small and in danger of dying out. The Chinese government may move some of the remaining pandas to sanctuaries in an attempt to establish new populations. One positive development is that the Chinese government has enacted laws to protect pandas, and the laws are being strictly enforced. However, because these unique bears eat only bamboo, a forest fire or a plant disease that killed bamboo trees could eliminate their food supply. If this happened, the pandas would simply disappear.

Polar bears are a tourist attraction in Churchill, Manitoba. Sometimes the bears are curious about the people as well!

In North America, the conservation of all three species of bears—polar, grizzly, and black—is based on many years of research. Although we need more information, we do know enough now to protect them in most of their present ranges. In several areas, bears may still be hunted legally, but illegal hunting is a continuing, and perhaps a growing, threat.

In some places where bears were exterminated in the past, they have been reintroduced. In Arkansas, for example, most black bears were eliminated by the early 1920s. In the 1960s and 1970s, 268 black bears, captured alive in Michigan, Saskatchewan, and Manitoba, were released in Arkansas. The bears were protected so they were able to survive and reproduce successfully. Now black bears are abundant again in Arkansas.

The best success story in bear conservation is that of the polar bear. In the 1960s, too many polar bears were being killed. There was international concern that they might become endangered, so scientists got together from all the countries that had polar bears: Canada, Denmark, Norway, the United States, and the Soviet Union. They agreed to work together, and in 1973, the five countries signed the International

On the vast, remote ice fields of the Arctic, polar bears still roam undisturbed by humankind.

Agreement on the Conservation of Polar Bears. As a result, polar bear populations are secure throughout the Arctic.

It is probably still possible to save all the bear species of the world, but time is running out for some of them. They need large areas of wild country in order to survive, and such places are becoming less and less common every day. One of the most important aspects of bear conservation is simply for humans to learn to coexist with bears. Conflicts between people and bears must be reduced. Sometimes that means just giving the bears a little extra consideration or a bit more space because there is nowhere left for them to retreat to.

To most people, bears are symbolic of true wilderness. In a world that humans are rapidly changing, a place that still has wild bears is special to all of us.

INDEX

Numbers in italics refer to photographs.

Age determination, 40
Alaska, bears in, 15, 16, 38, 39, 56, 58
American black bears, *16*, 16, *20*, 28
    habitats, *22–23*
    size and weight, 14
Arctic, bears in, 6–9, 12, 15, 27, 56
Asia, bears in, 15, 19, 59
Asiatic black bears, *16*, 16, *21*, 28, *47*
    habitats, *22–23*
    size and weight, 14

Bear family tree, 28
Bear population, 56
Bears,
    in Alaska, 15, 16, 38, 39, 50, 56, 58
    in Alberta, 56
    in Arctic, 6–9, 12, 15, 27, 56
    in Asia, 15, 19, 59
    behavior of, 10
    birth of, 30–32
    black. *See* Black bears
    breeding, 30
    in British Columbia, 15, 16, 50
    brown, 15
    in California, 56
    camping near, 60
    cave, 25
    in China, 12, *13*, 61
    communication by, 46–50
    dawn, 25
    determining age of, 40
    diet, 12, 15, 19, 27, 33–36, 37, 41–44
    early/first, 24, 25–29
    in Europe, 15, 25, 56
    female, 12, 14, 30–32, 37, 39, 52
    fishing by, 34–35, 42
    future for, 56–62
    giant short-faced, 26
    grizzly. *See* Grizzly bears
    habitats, 8, 9, 12–19, *22–23*, 25, 26, 56
    hibernation by, 54–55
    home ranges, 37–40
    human impact on, 56–62
    hunting by, 8, 34–36, 42
    in India, 19, 43
    in Labrador, 16
    male, 12, 14, 37, 39
    as mammals, 10
    maturity, 40

    in North America, 26, 56, 58
    panda. *See* Panda bears
    polar. *See* Polar bears
    sense of smell, 35, 45, 50
    similarity to humans, 10, 11
    sloth. *See* Sloth bears
    small, 28
    sounds, 47, 48–49
    in South America, 19
    species of, 12–23
    spectacled. *See* Spectacled bears
    in Sri Lanka, 19, 43
    stories of, 10
    sun, 14, *18*, 19, *48*
    survival of, 6, 32–40, 56–62
    teeth, 10, 25, 40, 41, 43, 44
    tracking by satellite, 39
    walking, 10, 12
    in winter, 52–55
    in Yellowstone National Park, 15
    young, 37. *See also* Cubs
Bear tracks, 17
Behavior, 10
Birth, 30–32
Black bears, 16–19, *30*, 30, *42*, *46*, *47*, 61
    American, 14, *16*, 16, *20*, *22–23*, 28
    Asiatic, 14, *16*, 16, *21*, *22–23*, 28, *47*
    compared with grizzly, 17
    future, 61
    size and weight, 14
    in winter, 52, 55
Breeding, 30, *31*
British Columbia, bears in, 15, 16
Brown bears, 15, 56

California, bears in, 56
Camping in bear country, 60
Cave bears, 25, 28
China, bears in, *13*, 61
Claws, 17, 49, 59
Coat, *26*
Collars, radio, 39
Communication, 46–50
Conservation, 56–62
Conservation of Polar Bears,
    International Agreement on the, 61–62
Cubs, 8–9, 9, *30*, 30–36, *32*, *33*, *34*, *35*, *49*, *51*; *See also* Young bears

Dawn bears, 25, 28
Dens, winter, 52–53
Diet, 12, 15, 19, 33–36, 37, 41–44
Digitigrade walking, 10

Early bears, 24, 25–29
Endangerment/extinction, 56–62
Europe, bears in, 15, 25, 56
European cave bears, 28

Face, shape of, 17
Family tree, bear, 28
Female bears, 12, 14, 30–32, 37, 39, 52
First bears, 25–29
Fishing, 34–35, 42
Florida cave bears, 28
Food, 12, 15, 19, 33–36, 37, 41–44
Fossils of early bears, 24, 27

Giant short-faced bears, 26, 28
Grizzly bears, 15, *17*, 28, 56, 58
    compared with black bear, 17
    future, 56–57, 61
    habitats, *22–23*
    home ranges, 38
    hunting, 42
    size and weight, 14
    in winter, 52, 54

Habitats, 8, 9, 12–19, *22–23*, 25, 26, 56
Hibernation, 54–55
Home ranges, 37–40
Hudson's Bay Company, 56
Human/bear similarities, 10, 11
Human impact on bears, 56–62
Hump, shoulder, 17
Hunting, 8, 34–36, 42, 56, 59, 61

India, bears in, 19, 43
International Agreement on the Conservation of Polar Bears, 61–62

Labrador, bears in, 16
Litters, 31

Male bears, 12, 14, 37, 39
Mammals, bears as, 10
Markings, communicating by, 47–48
Mating, 30, *31*
Maturity, 40

Native peoples, 10

63

681008

Neanderthals, 25
Neck, 26
North America, bears in, 26, 56, 58

Pakistan, bears in, 19
Panda bears, 12, 13, 21, 28, 43
  diet, 43
  future, 61
  habitats, 22–23
  home ranges, 38
  red, 51
  similarity to raccoons, 51
  size and weight, 14
Paws, 26, 29, 29, 50
Plantigrade walking, 10
Polar bears, 27, 28
  birth, 30
  diet, 44
  future, 61–62
  habitats, 22–23
  home ranges, 37–38
  International Agreement on the
    Conservation of, 61–62
  paws, 29

size and weight, 14
watching, 6–9
in winter, 52–53

Raccoons, 12, 52
Radio collars, 39
Ranges, home, 37–40
Red pandas, 51
Ringed seals, 44

Satellite, tracking bears by, 39
Seals, ringed, 44
Sense, of smell, 35, 45, 50
Size, communicating by, 46–47
Sizes and weights, 14
Sleep, winter, 52–55
Sloth bears, 19, 19, 21, 28
  diet, 43
  habitats, 22–23
  size and weight, 14
Small bears, 28
Smell, sense of, 35, 45, 50
Sounds, bear, 47, 48–49
South America, bears in, 19

Species of bears, 12–23
Spectacled bears, 19, 20, 24, 28
  diet, 44
  habitats, 22–23
  size and weight, 14
Sri Lanka, bears in, 19, 43
Sun bears, 18, 19, 20, 28, 48
  diet, 44
  habitats, 22–23
  size and weight, 14
Survival, 6, 32–40, 56–62

Teeth, 10, 25, 40, 41, 43, 44, 51, 59
Toes, 17
Tracking, 39
Tracks, 17
Trails, 50
Trees, 49

Walking, 10, 12
Winter sleep, 52–55

Yellowstone National Park, bears in, 15
Young bears, 37. See also Cubs

681088